Cross Stitch

Seaside Portraits

2

5

Stitch these enchanting designs for the little ones in your life!

Designs by Michele Johnson

LEISURE ARTS, INC. • Maumelle, Arkansas

Seaside Boy

Like beautiful paintings worked in floss on fabric, this serene portrait features a timeless elegance and gentle charm.

Stitch Count = 91w × 153h

FABRIC SIZE

- One 13" × 17" (33.0cm × 43.2cm) piece of 32-ct. Ice Blue Belfast® Linen by Zweigart® (stitched over 2 threads)

DESIGN SIZE

- 28-ct. = 6 1/2" × 11" (16.5cm × 27.9cm)
- 32-ct. = 5 5/8" × 9 1/2" (14.3cm × 24.1cm)
- 36-ct. = 5" × 8 1/2" (12.7cm × 21.6cm)

CROSS STITCH

ANCHOR		DMC	COLOR
002	☆	White	White
1038	5	519	Sky Blue
886	Λ	677	Very Light Old Gold
926	▽	712	Cream
361	H	738	Very Light Tan
387	8	739	Ultra Very Light Tan
275	[symbol]	746	Off White
359	C	801	Dark Coffee Brown
1034	S	931	Medium Antique Blue
1033	E	932	Light Antique Blue
881	4	945	Tawny
1010	T	951	Light Tawny
391	3	3033	Very Light Mocha Brown
1031	U	3753	Ultra Very Light Antique Blue
1037	○	3756	Ultra Very Light Baby Blue
1009	⊙	3770	Very Light Tawny
1008	A	3773	Medium Desert Sand

BACKSTITCH

ANCHOR		DMC	COLOR
890	—	729	Medium Old Gold
1035	—	930	Dark Antique Blue
1034	—	931	Medium Antique Blue
1008	—	3773	Medium Desert Sand

Bright pink area indicates last row of previous section of design.

TOP

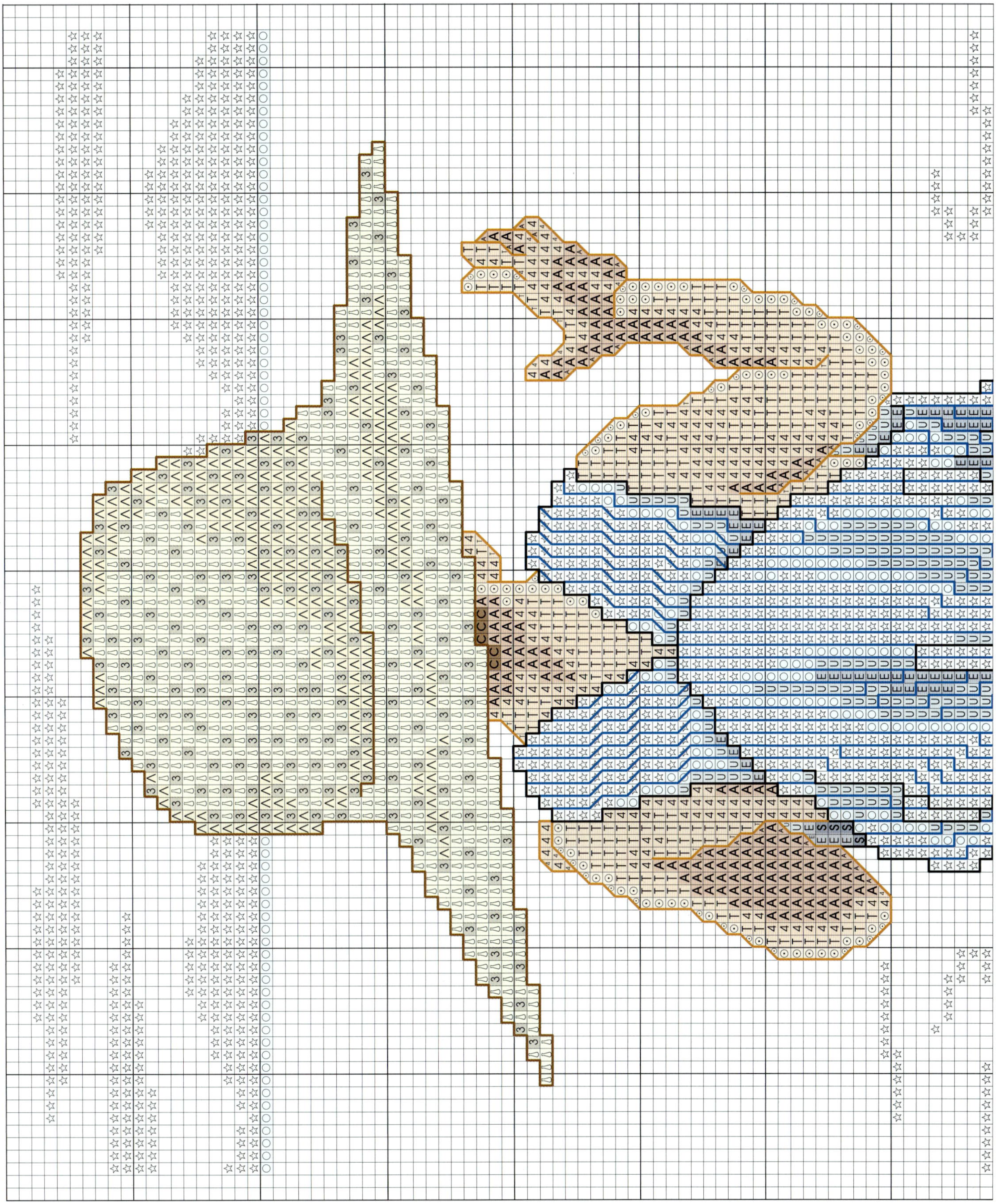

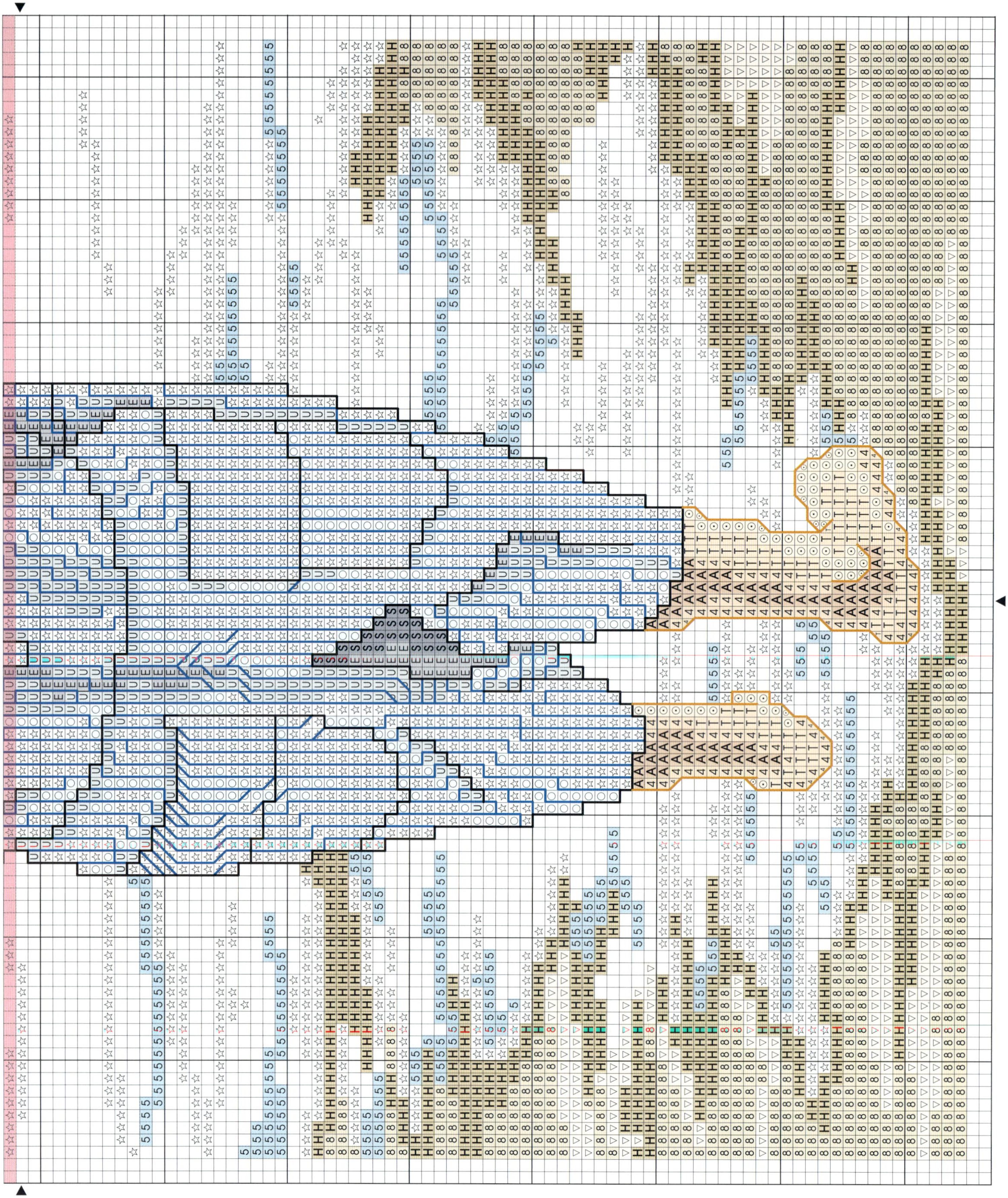

Seaside Girl

This endearing design captures the innocence of youth and the joy of first discoveries.

Stitch Count = 91w × 153h

FABRIC SIZE

- One 13" × 17" (33.0cm × 43.2cm) piece of 32-ct. Ice Blue Belfast® Linen by Zweigart® (stitched over 2 threads)

DESIGN SIZE

- 28-ct. = 6 1/2" × 11" (16.5cm × 27.9cm)
- 32-ct. = 5 5/8" × 9 1/2" (14.3cm × 24.1cm)
- 36-ct. = 5" × 8 1/2" (12.7cm × 21.6cm)

CROSS STITCH

ANCHOR		DMC	COLOR
002	☆	White	White
310	?	434	Light Brown
1045	Y	436	Tan
1038	5	519	Sky Blue
926	▽	712	Cream
361	H	738	Very Light Tan
387	8	739	Ultra Very Light Tan
359	C	801	Dark Coffee Brown
1034	S	931	Medium Antique Blue
1033	E	932	Light Antique Blue
881	4	945	Tawny
1011	6	948	Very Light Peach
1010	T	951	Light Tawny
1031	U	3753	Ultra Very Light Antique Blue
1037	○	3756	Ultra Very Light Baby Blue
1009	⊙	3770	Very Light Tawny
1008	A	3773	Medium Desert Sand

BACKSTITCH

ANCHOR	DMC	COLOR
359	801	Dark Coffee Brown
1034	931	Medium Antique Blue
1008	3773	Medium Desert Sand

Bright pink area indicates last row of previous section of design.

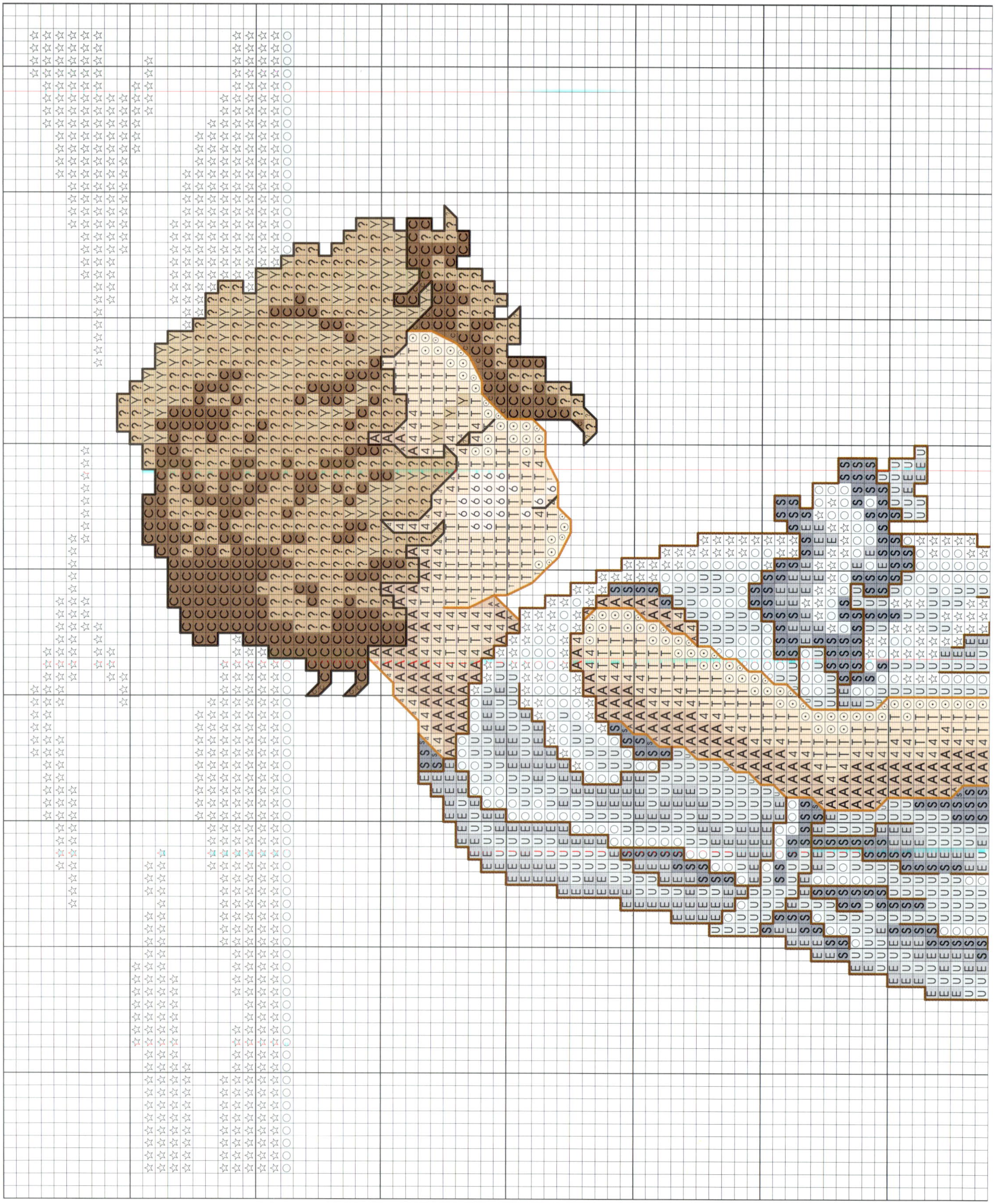

TOP ▶

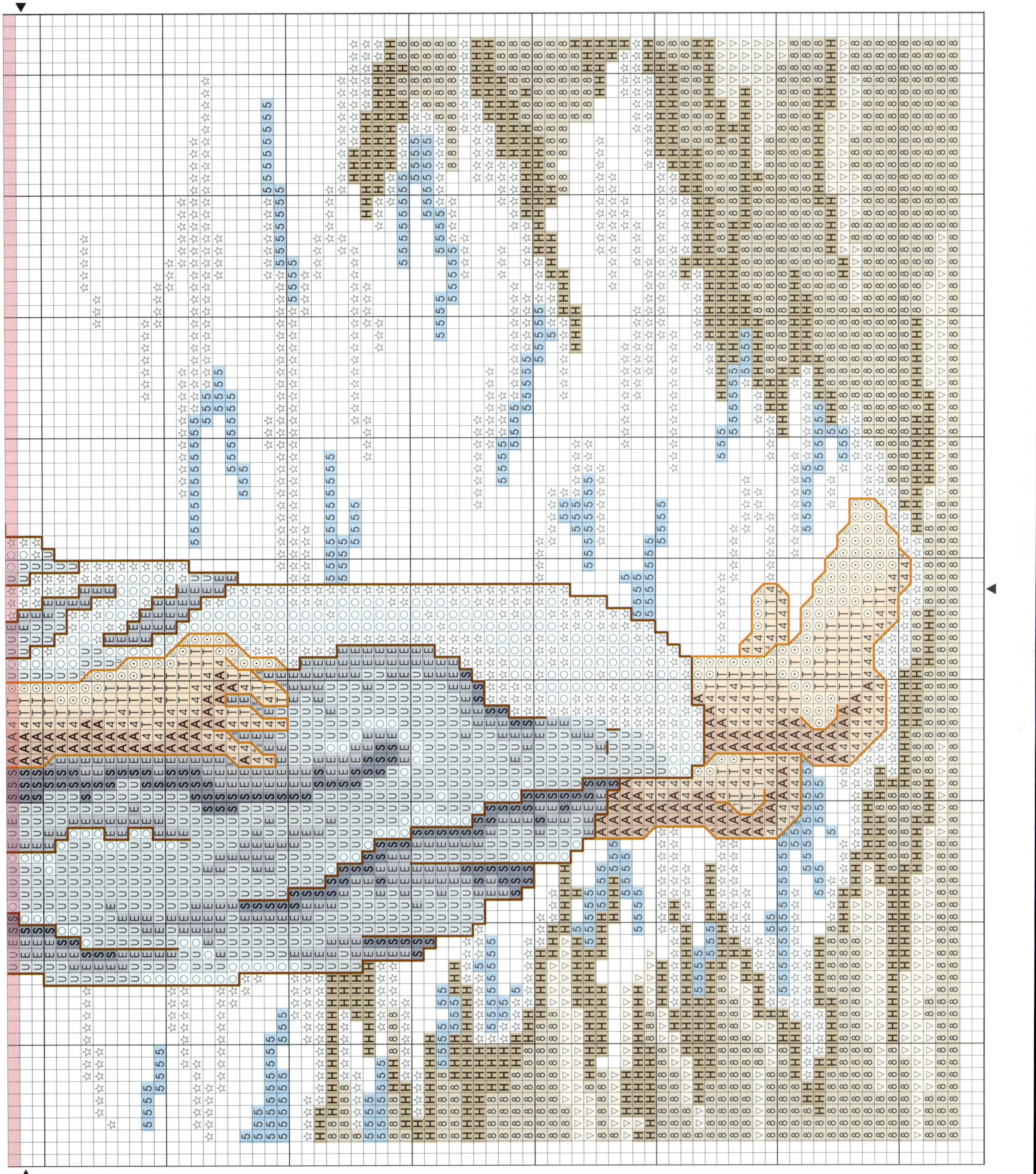

General Instructions

Getting Started

For most projects, the starting point is at the center. Every chart has arrows that indicate the horizontal and vertical centers. With your finger, trace along the grid to the point where the two centers meet. Compare a symbol at the center of the chart to the key and choose which floss color to stitch first. To find the center of the fabric, fold it into quarters and finger-crease.

Cut the floss into 15" lengths and separate all six strands. Recombine the appropriate number of strands and thread them into a blunt-tip needle. Use two strands of floss to work cross stitches and quarter stitches, and use one strand of floss to work backstitches.

To Secure Thread at the Beginning

The most common way to secure the beginning tail of the thread is to hold it on the wrong side of the fabric under the first four or five stitches.

To Secure Thread at the End

To finish, slip the threaded needle under previously stitched threads on the wrong side of the fabric for four or five stitches, weaving the thread back and forth a few times. Clip the thread.

Framing Your Pieces

Iron the finished needlework on the wrong side using a dry pressing cloth and medium temperature setting; do not steam. Accurately measure the length and width of your completed piece before purchasing a mat or frame. Consulting a professional framer or art supply store to mat and frame your design is recommended.

Cross Stitch

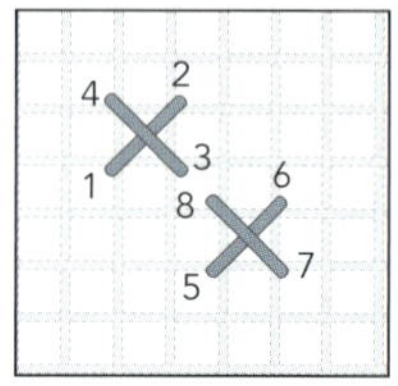

Make one cross stitch for each symbol on the chart. For horizontal rows, stitch the first diagonal of each stitch in the row. Work back across the row, completing each stitch. On most linen and evenweave fabrics, work the stitches over two threads as shown in the diagram. For aida cloth, each stitch fills one square. You also can work cross stitches in the reverse direction. Remember to embroider the stitches uniformly—that is, always work the top half of each stitch in the same direction.

Quarter Cross Stitches

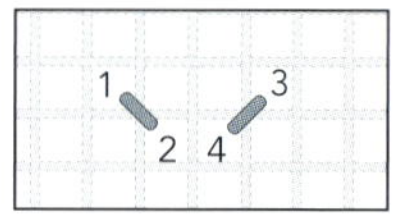

To obtain rounded shapes in a design, use quarter and three-quarter cross stitches. On linen and evenweave fabrics, a quarter stitch will extend from the corner to the center intersection of the threads. To make quarter cross stitches on aida cloth, estimate the center of the square.

Backstitches

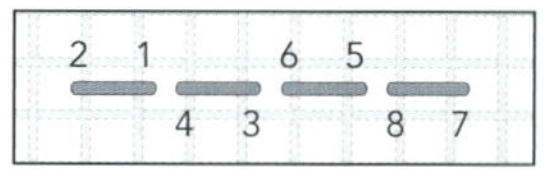

Working from right to left, bring the needle up from the back side of the fabric, one stitch length from your starting point. Begin the next stitch by inserting the needle at your starting point and back up two stitch lengths away. Continue, keeping all the stitches the same length.

Produced by Herrschners, Inc., for distribution exclusively by Leisure Arts, Inc., 104 Champs Blvd., STE 100, Maumelle, AR 72113-6738, leisurearts.com.